Looking Back, Looking Forward

Cody Somerville

BookLeaf Publishing

India | USA | UK

Presentation by *BookLeaf Publishing*

Web: www.bookleafpub.com

E-mail: info@bookleafpub.com

ISBN: 978-93-5744-946-5

First edition 2022

DEDICATION

To my family, partner, close friends and relatives.

PREFACE

Thank you for purchasing this book. I hope you enjoy reading it, as much as I enjoyed creating it.

This book contains 19 poems that have been individually created by myself. Each poem links to either "looking back" at some of my most fond memories of my life, or "looking forward" to the future that lies ahead in my life. Some of the themes you will find in this book are love, sport, music, leisure, hope, resilience, sadness and humour. My life has been filled with ups and downs, laughter, drama, celebration, tragedy and so many more elements. But these elements have also led to me thinking about what the rest of my life might look like. We always worry about the future, I know I certainly do. I have no idea what will happen, but my past experiences that I have looked back on, have led to me believing that there is always something to look forward to.

I hope you can connect to my poetry, no matter what your background or personality is. There are lots of different ideas being conveyed in this book. In the end, this is my story and I challenge you to think about your own after you finish reading.

Rhymes for the Reader

If you're reading this, I sincerely thank you
You're currently reading my first poem of this
book
To be given an opportunity to publish my first
ever collection of works
Is something that I could not overlook

A lot of the poems you're about to read
Are based on experiences I've encountered
throughout my life
Some are highlights and things to celebrate
Others are moments where I have been in strife

But some of the poems are also about the future
Even though I have no idea what is ahead for me
I always dream about what could possibly
happen
But in the end, my only option is to wait and see.

In one way or another, I hope you can connect
To what I'm writing and what I'm conveying

Because everyone has their own unique story to
tell
And everyone has their own cat and mouse
game they're playing

This is very relevant to me
Because like all of us, I'm very different to you
But all of these stories and feelings portrayed in
this book
Are straight from the heart, and very true

So I hope you enjoy this collection of works
And once again I thank you thoroughly
I aspire to inspire you with my views and
thoughts
I also hope I inspire you, to even have a go at
writing poetry

Senses of Stockton

I see coastal paradise
All along the waterfront
I see surfers searching for waves
Like they're on a treasure hunt
I see a community
Serving and loving their town
I see the horizon
Over the beach at sundown

I smell the weeds
That comes directly from the sea
I smell the catch of the day
Cooked and served up for tea
I smell the coal and woodchip
From the bypassing ships
I smell the takeaway shops
Frying freshly cut chips

I taste the saltiness
All day and all night long
I taste a seafood basket
The flavours are all so strong
I taste the bitterness
From a cold beer in the sun
I taste the sunscreen

I accidentally rubbed on my tongue

I hear people laughing
In town and on the beach
I hear the horns from the ships
That sound like a dreadful screech
I hear the crashing waves
From the waterfront and from the dock
I hear the bowlo's entertainment
It sounds like 80's pop rock

I feel the sand crumbling
On the bottom of my feet
I feel the pain of sunburn
Due to the great, yet harsh heat
I feel the entrance into water
It sends shivers down my spine
I feel at home when I'm in Stockton
It's a feeling that's most divine

A Poem for Past, Present, and Future Teachers

There are people in this world today
Who nurture our children's attributes and features
They gain their trust and find ways to maximise their potential
Yes, that's right! The people I'm talking about are our teachers

Teachers don't just stand at the front of a classroom
And lecture every child that is present
They take time to unlock the whole child
And make their learning experiences pleasant

Teachers don't just work from 9 to 3
They work from dawn until even later
They are the people who think about their class when they go to sleep
To see how they can make their education greater

Teachers don't just teach for the money
They teach because they commit themselves
everyday
To helping the next generation of kids grow
Through learning, laughter, and play

Teachers don't just do it for the holidays
In fact, the holidays are not a time for a break
It's a time to think about the next stage of their
class' learning
Holidays for teachers are not a piece of cake

As a teacher myself, I'm blessed I'm given this
opportunity
To make a difference in a life of a child
To be a role model and leader of the way
And a person that allows their students'
imagination to run wild

So to all of the past teachers, I thank you
For your effort over your career
Whether it was one or many years of your life
You have given your ex-students something to
cheer

To our present teachers, I thank you
You're responsible for educating our next
generation

Continue to have passion for this truly unique
career
Because in a child's eyes, you're their sensation

To our future teachers, I welcome you
And look forward to what you will innovate
Because you will have the big responsibility
Of continuing to teach our world's children, and
continuing to make learning great.

When I'm 50

To my 50-year old self,

I hope you're okay
I hope you're well and healthy
I hope your wife and children are safe
I hope your bank account looks wealthy

I hope you still play music
I hope you still feel young
I hope you still go swimming
I hope you still have fun

I hope you feel happy
But also feel sad sometimes
I hope you stay active
But also rest up sometimes

I hope you still love your job
I hope you still have many friends
I hope you still visit your parents
I hope you reflect once each day ends

Because even when you're 50
You can still keep being you

And being you is such a great thing to do
I know for certain, that is very true

Yours sincerely,
You

My Favourite Drug

Ever since I was 6
I have been addicted to this one drug
It keeps me alive and well 24/7
And prevents me from having a stomach bug

I was told if I don't have it, I would die
So I kept on giving it to myself
To this day, I'm still here living the dream
And maintaining my overall health

This drug helps control my blood sugar
It's stops me from going too high
I still can't fathom how I got to this
I'm still searching for the reasons why?

No one in my family has what I have
But I guess I can't procrastinate anymore
Because if I forget to give myself this drug
I might just end up on the floor

If I was to go back in time
I would ask Merlin to perform a spell
So that this state of mine could be removed
And this so-called disease in my cells

However, that is not possible
So I have to think about my life ahead
I hope I keep receiving my favourite drug
If not, I'll find myself in a hospital bed

So to my favourite drug, I thank you
For giving me a chance to live
To anyone else who has these similar symptoms
You should thank this drug too
Because without it, our life may not be
something we can forgive

A Profile of Dogs

Jack
Golden, Fluffy
Rolling, playing, barking
An even tempered character
Affectionate

Jess
Golden, Smooth
Socialising, loving, caring
An ideal loyal protector
Companion

Rosie
Energetic, Aware
Sprinting, hunting, loving
A curious natural explorer
Foxie

Gip,
Elegant, Attentive
Listening, running, jumping
An agile problem solver
Smart

Pathogenic Times

Our world currently has a global pandemic
Which started as a low-key epidemic
It originated in China
And then it spread via
The rest of the globe, it indeed is pathogenic

In a short matter of time
The virus hit its prime
Thousands of people became sick
Because the pandemic spread quick
And leaving your home became a crime

It indeed was a wake-up call
For families, for businesses, for all
Our lives changed as quick as lightning
Being surrounded by sickness is still frightening
We were apart of the world's largest fall

As case numbers increased
Our time outside decreased
We Zoomed in for meetings
And used video call for greetings
Sadly, some people with the virus became
deceased

It's been almost 2 years since the first case
Finally in Australia, we're on the stretch to
home base
Many individuals have received a vaccine
And more people are keeping their hands clean
And we are back to seeing each other
face-to-face

This is no doubt, the biggest health problem we
have ever seen
But whenever a person asks me "how have you
been?"
I always reply "Thanks for asking mate"
"I'm doing really great"
Even though we are still living with the
continuous threat… of COVID-19.

Are you okay?

Are you okay?
It's a question we can easily ask
Yet only a few can easily answer
It can draw emotion or a response
Or it can cause a deflection and no response
Yet this is a question we should ask everyone…
everyday.

We can't always read minds like psychics
Hence why our only way of unlocking the status
of those in our lives
Is to ask them "are you okay?"
This question gives them a sense of hope
That their voice can be heard
And can be listened to

However, it can also backfire
Anxiety can be a person's worst enemy at times
It limits the potential to express someone's
emotion
Sometimes people feel like they can't speak up
Like an individual with a communication barrier
Yet the only barrier apparent is their self-esteem.

This is why we should all remember
That we can't judge a book by its cover
We have to dive deeper into those who are
around us
Over 3 million people have anxiety and
depression
And I bet a large percentage have not come
forward
To respond to a question that matters to many
Are you okay?

A Famous Tackle

2016 was a year to remember
A time of stress, a time of celebration
Exams, drinking, and transition to manhood
A time that caused a lot of emotional elation

Yet there was one event that stood out to me
That took place on the second of October
The event occurred after the final whistle
An event, that occured whilst I was not sober

The shire just celebrated a grand final victory
All the beers kept going down like lemonade
My drunk self was starting to become apparent
I'm surprised no one came to my aid

My mate Bucko looked at me and stared,
He said "run straight at me with a ball in hand"
This guy is a lot stronger and agile
But I agreed to the challenge and took a stand

I positioned myself outside on the grass
Holding the ball and ready to run
Bucko took hold on the other side
Eager to get rough and consider me "done"

My other friends started recording on their
phones
Whilst I sprung off my step towards my rival
I ran straight, but then I suddenly stopped
Clenching the ball in hand for survival

I found myself up in the air
Then came back down at a glance
I hit the ground with impact
I bet Bucko knew I didn't stand a chance

The recording ended up being posted
To a rugby league page on Facebook
The tackle between Bucko and I became famous
Over 40 thousand people had a look

To this day I still remember 2016
A year I celebrated and cherished
But that famous tackle still jogs my memory
A night where my whole body perished

On the Football Field

It is game day down at the club oval
The crowds fill up with all of the locals
The goalposts are up and the oranges are peeled
For the two teams contesting on the football
field

The players gather around with their coach
To discuss attack, defence and their tactical
approach
Their opponents are also having a shout
About how they can win and close the game out

The whistle blows for the start of the game
The teams play hard early, to state their claim
There is no other option then to win
And give one-hundred percent, through thick
and thin

Once a goal is scored, momentum changes
And pressure can creep in like a bunch of
strangers

Yet the crowd motivates the conceding team to
stop being slack
And find the inner strength to achieve a
comeback

The gameplay in football can be so sublime
That anything can change, anywhere and
anytime
As long as each player is fulfilling their role
There will always be a chance to score a goal

At half time, the teams receive some feedback
By their coach, who discusses both the defence
and the attack
Sometimes, half time is important for both sides
As there is an opportunity to maintain or change
the tides

The second half is an exciting part
Both teams are challenged to show true strength
and heart
To not allow their physical and mental game
become thinner
So that they can defend their lead or score the
winner

At full-time, it's either win, lose or draw
The teams shake hands, no matter the result or
score

Then they passionately celebrate the sport they
yield
And manifest their performance on the football
field

Identity

Identity, A word that means many things
It can range from our date and place of birth
From gender, to appearance, family background
and race
And our existence on planet Earth
The identity of the human person can change
over time
As we become older, we are more
coming-of-age
When we finish school, we go into the real
world
And our purpose of life begins a new stage
While we live, there's one thing we have to
know
We must never leave our old identity behind
But now our bright future lies ahead for us
We'll never know what our identity will find

19 Reasons Why I Love You

On the 19th September 2019
You became my other half
And since that day we have done may things
Such as kiss, hug, cry and laugh

Like any relationship, friendship turns into like
And like turns into love
So here are 19 things about you
19 things about you that I love

You're down to earth
Like a chest full of treasure
You have a smile that makes me smile
And lips that give me pleasure

You put heart into every meal
Hence why I find your food delicious
You're so gentle and kind
And never malicious

You have a voice of an angel
Even when your vocals are tone deaf

But everytime you say you love me
It takes my breath away

Your hugs are as cuddly as a teddy
But 1000 times greater
And even if you don't give me a massage now
You always keep your promise and do it later

Your eyes are precious
And so is your butt
You take care of me when I'm sick
And treat every bite, bruise and cut

Even when I act strange, you still appreciate me
You tell me when I'm doing the wrong thing
You're a teacher just like me
And you listen to everybody, and everything

But the 19th reason why I love you
Is the most important of all nineteen
It is the fact that your overall personality
And your overall appearance
Is the most beautiful thing I've ever met and
ever seen

Heavy Rain

Heavy rain falls again
Across the coast and the western plains
Every drop soaks up the dirt
As well as your shoes and T-Shirt

Heavy rain through the night
Keeps dry land out of sight
In the west everybody prays
For the showers to last for days

Heavy rains brings the flood
And turns dirt into puddles of mud
It soaks up the moisture in the ground
So that our veggie gardens can come around

Heavy rain keeps the sun away
And let's the land grow day after day
All the life stock, plants and sugar cane
Keep us all alive due to heavy rain

Look Beyond the Boundaries

People often worry about the possibility
That their newborn child may have a disability
Well in 1999, that was the case for my mother
and father
Because special needs were detected within my
beloved brother

Growing up, I knew our life would continue to
change
However, I still didn't understand why he was
acting strange
Tantrums, impatience, communication barriers
and endless tears
Kept on going like a highway for many years

But when I turned 9, he was enrolled in a special
school
An education setting with sensory classrooms,
facilities and a pool
It was a place for students with severe
disabilities and needs

Yet it's a place where they're given a chance to
grow and succeed

After a year, our family already saw a lead
He was able to learn how to read
This followed on with counting up to 30
And communication through a device and typing
on a QWERTY

My strange brother was not becoming so strange
after all
He was growing in his education and was also,
growing tall
My parents also set high expectations everyday
If he responded positively, he would be
rewarded with play

Before we knew it, he transitioned to senior
school
Like the last one, this one also had sensory areas
and a pool
The teachers guided Robbie to significant
success every year
That he was given an opportunity to have a
career

From a little boy who was thought to have no
hope

Is now using machines and packaging boxes of
soap
From a little boy who was filled with sadness
and frustration
Is now a person who is full of smiles and elation

This has happened through lots of love that was
tough
And a lot of what he went through was rough
As a person with a disability, he still has a
forever challenge to face
Yet becoming more independent is something he
won't have to erase

I guess the moral of this story is to always
believe
Because if you don't, there is no opportunity to
achieve
Always look beyond the boundaries that
yourself or somebody might possess
Because no matter who you are, there is always
potential for success

Burger Poem

In our world of cult heroes and classics
There is one food that separates from all
And that is a fresh juicy hamburger
That has exquisite ingredients and stands tall

It all starts with the juicy beef
That is seasoned with pepper and salt
Then seared on a piping hot grill
That makes the patty sizzle and jolt

And might I just add, the layers are key
As well as a slice of cheddar cheese
Tomato, lettuce, onion and beetroot
With BBQ sauce… oh yes please!

But a burger can't be complete
Without two buns made of fresh bread
And once you cut into the middle
The beef is good when its slightly red

Once the burger is set
You chop up some spuds to make fries
Once they're lowered into the deep fryer
They start to go gold like a meat pie

Serve on a yellow plastic plate
And get ready to take a big bite
Hold with two hands and make eye contact
Before you experience a real delight

The flavours all start to explode
They're all as powerful as a punch
But the flavour of the beef is sensational
As well as the bun, by which you crunch

The salty fries cannot be forgotten
As well as the sauce within the package
And when it's all over, I feel full
Like my stomach is full of excess baggage

I cannot wait to eat a Rascal's burger again
Because every time I do it feels like a dream
Beef, tomato, lettuce, onion, sauce and a bun
With a side of fries… wow, that is a real team!

Joe Blow

*This is not a poem about me. However, the
message is something I'd still like to spread*

In 1950, Joe Blow was born
The same year the Korean War began
He grew up fast, and loved wearing Buster
Browns
As well as eating Benedict peas from a can

By the time Joe entered the 1960s,
He loved music, and was a Beatles fan
But he hated school, because of the cane
So he left in Year 10, and became a delivery man

Joe's fashion changed during the 70s
Nehru jackets and turtlenecks were his thing
But his habits dramatically changed too
Winnie Blues tempted Joe to start smoking

By the 80s, he was a party man
Dancing at the club singing Livin On A Prayer
He changed his job to a day shift steelworker
And was saddened to hear the death of Fred
Estaire

Joe started to slow down in the 90s
He purchased his very own computer by Dell
Nirvana rocked his world, and so did his Nike's
But the world kept changing, and he could tell

Joe felt like a stranger in the new millennium
Especially when he was gifted an iPhone
Hip Hop didn't appeal to him, unlike rock'n'roll
And watching Lord of the Rings was different to
watching Home Alone

In 2010, Joe felt alienated by the rest of the
world
Phones were taking over, instead of playing
outside
He did enjoy streaming old movies on Netflix
And taking his Hyundai i30 for a ride

However, by the beginning of 2020
He felt like this purpose hasn't been fulfilled
After hearing too much about Tiktok and Covid
He was definitely far from thrilled

Joe Blow lived for 71 years
For a lot of those years, he was glad
But once the 21st century hit
His perspective on life turned awfully bad

The moral of the story is to challenge yourself
Despite how much the world changes each year
Learn to adapt instead of find a way out
So you can live in happiness, instead of fear

A Musical Journey (#n.b.foronelasthoor ah?)

Music is my greatest talent
I've known since I plucked my first guitar
I nurture every song
By which I sing along
I knew with music, I could go far

My hobby started at Genr8
Then moved to Rosie's School of Rock
Rock is electric
And singing is authentic
I learned both every Monday at 6 o'clock

This went on for a long while
Until school kicked in and took up time
I really missed the tunes
Because my afternoons
Usually featured playing and vocalising rhyme

Then I met another guitar teacher near home
He was like the next rockstar

I was happy again
I was out of my den
And back to hitting my golden crisp guitar

My mates from school played too
We formed a rock'n'roll band
We played some awesome gigs
To crowds, small and big
The love of music is something we all
understand

Once school ended we drifted apart
And we got real positions
But we still found the time
To compose a hard rhyme
Our musical journey was in a transition

Because we formed an indie group
That was busy and gained traction
We played with Newy's best
And performed out of our chest
The shows gave our lives some satisfaction

But now I'm sad, because it's gone
We drifted apart, again, in different places
Then we had to break up
It really gave me a shake up
That I couldn't see my band and best mates'
faces

I hope in the near distant future
That we have one last hoorah together
Because music is so great
Especially with my mates
They're moments I will cherish forever

Favourite Food Alphabet

Asparagus
Beef
Chicken
Duck
Egg
Fish
Garlic
Hazelnut
Ice cream
Jerky
Kangaroo
Lamb
Mango
Nutella
Octopus
Potato
Quiche
Rissoles
Sausage
Tomato
Udon
Veal

Whiting
Xigua
Yoghurt
Zucchini

Gift of Life Prayer

Dear Lord,
Thank you for the gift of life
I feel honoured that I get to experience what life
is all about
Without life, I cannot live by the word of the
Lord
Without life, I cannot be present with God and
our saviour Jesus Christ

I ask you Lord
To protect me, from the threat of danger that I
might encounter in my life
To forgive me, when I do wrong by others and
by you
To enlighten me, with the gift of the Holy Spirit
To teach me, how to live by the word of God and
apply it to everyday life
To love me, so that I can send love to others
To remember me, when the gift of life is no
longer a gift I have

May this prayer be heard and recognised, so that
I can fulfil and maintain the gift of life. I ask this
through Christ our Lord and Saviour

Amen.